Shouldn't She?

Nature's Gift to
Family Businesses

Naomi Njau-George

Published by Amazing Life Publishing House
P.O. Box 4002-01002, Thika, Kenya.
Tel: +254723285236
Email: info@amazinglifehouse.com
Website: https://amazinglifehouse.com

Mobile: +254700060681
naomigeorgew@gmail.com
© Amazing Life Publishing House, 2023

First published 2023

ISBN: 978-9914-9632-2-9

contents

dedication

This book is dedicated to three out of four members of the 'Greatest Family WhatsApp group', my best friends, Sir George, Stacy, and Victoria. I am honoured to be WhatsApp group member number four. I value your input. You are all true polymaths. I love you.

I further dedicate this piece to my loving Daddy, Mr. J.G. Kanyiri, a man who must have believed in me since my first day on earth. I have had to put in extra effort in all my endeavours over the years so that I don't let him down. May the Lord bless you, Daddy.

acknowledgements

To my two cousins, Irene Marubu and Dr. Peter Kamande, who double up as mentors, and whose leadership insights I have silently and unashamedly followed. You are my champions.

To my friend and mentor, Dr. Anne Ndirangu, you are a true source of inspiration, a role model for women in leadership. I appreciate you.

Sr. Jane Wakahiu, your words of encouragement at the Giraffe Hotel in Dar Es Salaam keep ringing in my mind, 'Women should embrace their natural ability of strategic and transformational leadership.' This inspired me a lot. You are a treasure to Africa and the world.

Growing up, when elders asked a younger person numerous questions, it meant that the person had disappointed them, and an explanation was required immediately. When Professor Dan Kiambi called me aside after a tense defence of my thesis, which had questions coming from every corner of the room, I was worried he would tell me how disappointed he was in me. He, however, challenged me to write a book since the topic had attracted a lot of interest among his colleagues; no wonder the many questions. Thanks for the challenge, Prof! This reconstructed piece has brought out all the lessons learnt from my research.

foreword

This book endeavours to highlight the role of women in running successful family businesses by objectively engaging different case studies that prove the hypothesis that they are more than able to do that. This pursuit is absolutely needed and welcome in an "African" society that traditionally tends to favour its men in giving (business) leadership opportunities and celebrating their achievements at the expense of their female counterparts.

The hypothesis is well formulated in three researchable questions/areas, namely, that of whether women are good leaders, whether by nature they are transformational, and how that transformational nature and mentorship of younger women leads to success in business. The positive findings are well interwoven within the transformational leadership theoretical approach to bring out its practicability and positive impact that is well demonstrated by the wholesome approach of women leadership which not only leads to the profitability of businesses but in the process, focuses on the welfare of workers as team players in that endeavour. The "down to earth" academic way of how the research is conducted and how the interviewees are objectively engaged in a very friendly environment, cunningly invites the reader to arrive at the same findings, thus putting the findings beyond doubt. This indeed is a classic demonstration of bridging the academia to respond to everyday situations.

What is exciting as one reads the book is the fact that the author's skills in business consulting, mainly that of motivating a team approach to achieving results, led to solutions that came up in the course of her research. I was personally excited to see the author's role as a facilitator as the parties involved in the case studies come up with workable solutions and share them with those undergoing the same challenges. The author's research quest was an opportunity to also help others move to the next level, which is very commendable.

The tone and style of the book are very appealing. Having been in academia for several years and reviewing theses from students, I expected a complicated reading that would normally end up, as many have, on library shelves. But the way the author has communicated her findings, even using humor in the process, makes this book "a cover-to-cover" reading for everyone who takes hold of it, whether in the formal or informal setting.

I recommend this book to many who still struggle with the question of whether a woman should be entrusted with running a business, or any other leadership role in society at large. The author has ably proved that when women are given a chance, they can use their natural (God-given) transformational skills to lead businesses into a "win-all" situation. I hope that at the end of reading this book, you will echo together with me in response to the question posed on the cover of the book, that indeed SHE SHOULD!

Peter Kamande Thuo, Ph.D.
Adjunct Faculty, School of Theology,
Pan Africa Christian University,
Nairobi, Kenya.

As a Master's student, I conducted research on the influence of transformational leadership on business performance; focusing on family businesses with women at the helm. After defending my thesis, Professor Dan Kiambi graciously called me aside, served me a cup of tea, and challenged me to write a book on this interesting topic. However, this became one of the things I pushed aside every time, with the excuse that I did not have enough time.

A time came when I urgently needed time off from my normal life. I needed a distraction! I am sure this sounds selfish, but doesn't the Holy Book say that some preach out of envy and rivalry, others out of goodwill ... but one way or the other, the important thing is that Christ is preached? Either way, this book was written too. I was down for days with accumulated fatigue from a political venture. I sure needed a distraction! Otherwise, I was going to slowly swim into depression.

This book became a welcome distraction. I hope to encourage women to take up leadership roles without fear or self-doubt. I am optimistic that men will also appreciate a world-view of transformational leadership from a woman's lens and consequently cheer their grandmothers, wives, daughters, nieces, cousins, and mothers to take up leadership.

introduction

My first experience vying for leadership was at the age of twenty in my second year in college. I had previously been a Bible study and Home Science Club leader in high school, but these were mere appointments. I vied for the position of secretary to the student leadership body. The outgoing team was completing college, and a new breed needed to come on board.

This was a season of pasting candidates' posters on every visible wall. I wrote what I thought could be done differently if I won. I moved from class to class, telling everyone what I would change. College life needed to feel great for every student! I had a vision, and this, I thought, would only be realised if I was in the leadership team. On the eve of the elections, I stood on stage in the vast dining hall dressed in my favourite brown skirt and a cream shirt. I had worn a pair of brown heels to boost my confidence; I had read in a magazine that heels keep a woman confident

I was slightly nervous but had to gather myself together. My two opponents, two brilliant ladies from my class, had what it took to win. One of them went first and gave her speech. She was eloquent and delivered a speech that made lots of sense. Everyone clapped for her. I clapped too. The second lady was next, and her speech was equally good. She got a standing ovation. When my turn came, I decided to make my speech less formal. I had watched politicians in the village engage the electorate. They made half statements, and the audience would shout out the remaining part to complete the sentence. They ensured they made the audience laugh and dance a bit. I needed to deviate from my opponents' formal academic speeches. I started by cracking a joke that got everyone laughing. I had figured out how to make half statements that would require them to complete the sentences in chorus. I also requested the DJ to play a song that got everyone up and dancing as I exited the stage.

I was not sure I had explained my vision on stage that day. I assumed the days I had visited all the classrooms and elaborated my vision would pay back. But later, I kept thinking about the speech and wondered if I should have kept it formal, like my colleagues. I felt that I had goofed. The students would be voting the following day. I was walking a thin rope. My only consolation was that I had lobbied a lot, especially among the members of the Christian Union, whose treasurer I had been for a while.

The following morning looked brighter than usual. The scorching sun came out quite early. Voting was done first thing in the morning. I was keen to be present as the clerks counted the votes. I didn't mind missing the first lesson.

The Chairman's votes were counted first. My friend won. I watched him receive the news of his win with much relief. The secretary's votes were next. I was sweating profusely. The clerks began by separating the votes of the three candidates. One of my colleague's heap of papers looked quite huge. I was almost certain she had won. It was counting time. They counted mine first. I had one thousand two hundred and four votes. They counted the next two piles of papers; one of my opponents had five hundred votes while the other had one thousand two hundred and one votes. I won! Narrowly though, but I got a ticket into the college leadership team.

 All fifteen student leaders held frequent meetings with the principal, dean of students, and Heads of Department. This made me feel very mature. I took the minutes (I wouldn't say I liked this part), and we laid down strategies for implementing changes (this was the part I enjoyed most).

An office near the canteen was designated for the chairman and me. This would give students easy access to us in case of challenges. This felt good. I spent most of my Saturday and Sunday afternoons at the office. It had two tables and two wooden chairs. We had to keep the lights on since the room lacked adequate natural light. This was, however, a good enough privilege. I realised leadership came with goodies, a bowl of responsibilities, and daily challenges. Our main job was to ensure calm and order within the institution. We needed to balance the students' needs, wants, and demands and the management's expectations, rules, and structures. It was not an easy job. But we left the college better than we found it. My vision was realised.

My nagging concern was that we only had three ladies out of the 15 leadership team members. Eighty percent were men. I may not remember the student population ratio of ladies to men in the college, but 20:80 was definitely not it. We had very few ladies vying for any leadership positions.

Worse, no lady attempted to compete for the chairman's position, while, on the other hand, no gentleman attempted to vie for the secretary's position. It seemed natural that the chair had to be a man and the secretary had to be a woman. Looking back, I wish I had vied for the chairman's position, but I am not sure I would have garnered substantial votes.

Are we really in the 21st century? Believe it or not, in this day and age, we still have people who believe that a woman's place at work is to be subordinate and that men should take the lead. As a young girl in the early 80s, I wondered why every primary school I knew or heard of in the village had a headmaster. Why not a head-madam? I cannot recall ever coming across the term 'headmistress' then. The young me replaced 'master' in headmaster with 'madam'.

At the age of ten, I thought headmasters were great leaders who brought real change in everyone's life, even beyond the confines of their schools. They were elected as chairmen in various committees; churches, cattle dips, weddings and burials. They were opinion shapers who influenced the tide of voting for political candidates. Our mothers and grandparents would

> *Believe it or not, in this day and age, we still have people who believe that a woman's place at work is to be subordinate and that men should take the lead.*

consult them about whom they should vote for as their political leader every time that season came by. It bothered me a lot that there were no women shaping opinions, at least none that I knew of. Leadership was seemingly a male domain, and this was quite disturbing.

Emmah topped my class in every exam. I kept wondering why she wouldn't be appointed as the class prefect. Our class prefect was a boy, yet many girls performed better than him academically. Why wouldn't they pick one of the bright girls? Wasn't a prefect supposed to be an all-round role model?

> *Why wouldn't they pick one of the bright girls? Wasn't a prefect supposed to be an all-round role model?*

From a child's point of view, my interest then was solely on gender. I experienced a really unfair under-representation of girls in leadership and was determined to change this when I grew up. I wished Emmah would one day be a head-madam and lead a school when we grew up. She was bright and had what it takes, or so I thought.

A lot has changed in organizational leadership since my primary school days. There has been a rallying call from all over the world to elevate women to leadership positions. However, the reality is that only a few organizations have heeded the call or embraced women as their leaders. Reading through numerous pieces of literature, I gathered that the number of women holding leadership positions globally within the family business sector in small and medium enterprises was only about 22 percent. Eighty-eight percent were men, with a majority of the women taking up menial roles. And yet, this was research conducted in 2017. In the 21st century; surely, we would expect different statistics.

I came across the term 'transformational leadership' during my coursework for graduate studies. It captivated me. It also felt to me like the natural way of life for women.

With a strong belief that a business is only as good as its leader, a few questions were triggered in my mind:

1. *Would women lead family businesses successfully?*

2. *Are women naturally transformational?*

3. *Would business mentorship of younger women lead to successful family businesses?*

These questions triggered my curiosity, and my journey to get answers began.

jacky disrupts
her father's business

A business opened its doors to the public to sell bulbs, torches, and lamps. Wanjihia had just returned from overseas and had put aside some savings. He needed to start and grow his business fast. While abroad, he worked for a company that specialized in selling lighting products. "Why not swim in familiar waters?" he wondered. He had a burning desire to catch up with his local friends and former classmates, who were now way ahead with rental units, homes for their families, and businesses that were scaling up profitably. Luckily, there was a market for his business concept. He registered Wanjihia Light Company Limited and kicked off. A name had to appear in the business name, and it had to be his, typical of business people in his culture. Most of his kinsmen actually just picked the first two letters of their names, their spouses' and firstborns' names to create a business name.

Wanjihia's wife, Njeri, and their daughter, Jacky, would have formed an ideal company name, Wanjeja Co. Ltd. This could be switched around to find the best one; Wajanje, Njewaja, Jawanje, Njejawa, Janjewa, and so on.

Wanjihia became synonymous with bulbs, torches, and lamps. He became a brand. Business was good. However, not without hitches - some key employees, who were good with customers, kept leaving, either for greener pastures or to start their own similar businesses. Over time, this brought Wanjihia's business down. Some of his previously loyal customers followed his former employees for cheaper goods without caring much about their quality. It was frustrating to recruit a new person, train and trust them enough to run the business while he was away, only to have them leave within no time.

 Njeri, Wanjihia's wife, who worked as a teacher in a secondary school, spent time at the business over the weekends. The high staff turnover disturbed her a lot, so she decided to conduct exit interviews. The constant feedback was that Wanjihia was too strict and did not recognise the hard work the employees put into the business. Most of them felt they had gone the extra mile many times, but Wanjihia would forget all their good deeds and fire them without warning whenever they made any slight mistake. They mentioned to Njeri that they lived in fear and that their jobs were not secure. Njeri waited for the right time to discuss the high turnover and exit interview results with her husband.

Jacky, Wanjihia's daughter, had just completed University, and instead of idling at home, her mother, Njeri, encouraged her to join the business. Wanjihia was initially hesitant but heeded his wife's request for the sake of peace. Njeri felt that Jacky could slowly take care of the employee turnover. She shared the results of the exit interviews with her daughter and sent her on a mission to ensure there was some level of retention. They had continued to lose key employees, resulting in a further downward spiral in sales and profits.

It was six o'clock on a chilly Monday morning. I knocked twice on the huge unwelcoming black gate. A heavily built security guard dressed in a khaki uniform opened the heavy gate with a single swing and smiled. I felt like an atom. His size gave me the David-Goliath experience. After exchanging pleasantries, I introduced myself politely and indicated that Madam Njeri had sent me. I was feeling a bit nervous. His size was undoubtedly intimidating. He let me know that they had been expecting me and led me inside. I filled in my details on his visitors' register, and he directed me to the main reception. Njeri had forewarned me that I needed to be at the premises very early if I intended to chat with her daughter. I hadn't taken breakfast yet, but I had a small red flask with some tea and a container with two slices of bread in my basket. I unashamedly took my breakfast at the reception. I smiled at some point when I thought of how age takes away shame. Taking your breakfast at someone's office reception would have been a no-no ten years ago. But now, at my age, hunger is handled 'as is where is.'

Dressed in a black pair of jeans and an orange t-shirt branded "Wanjihia's Lighting Co." was a tall, dark, pretty girl with a broad welcoming smile. It had to be Njeri's daughter. She bore a striking resemblance to her mother. On seeing her, I immediately remembered when young Njeri and I worked together in a training firm in the city. We were in our mid-twenties. Njeri was tall, dark, and pretty. She loved wearing jeans on Fridays, the only day that we were allowed to dress down. The only difference between Njeri then and her daughter, Jacky, was that the pants and tops we wore in our days had to be oversized. Our petite bodies whirled inside our clothes. This memory made me smile. The smile doubled for both Jacky as she shook my hand, and the memory in my mind. I quickly had to come back to the world of reality for time and tide wait for no man.

Jacky greeted me warmly and walked me to her tiny office. I was quick to notice a huge red duvet folded neatly and placed at the corner of the couch ... Does this young lady sleep in the office? I wondered. I had to make a choice not to focus on it. Nothing was going to distract me from my mission. I needed to know how Jacky had been doing since joining her dad's company. Her mother had tipped me off a bit.

The witty, shy girl wasn't sure she had much to say. She just kept saying, "We are good! We are good!" I probed on but realised I wasn't going to get much from her. Perhaps she was shy to talk about her accomplishments at the company. I requested to speak to a few members of the staff. She quickly agreed and seemed relieved that she would no longer be the centre of focus. She requested the general manager to join me and quickly excused herself. She went to the common room to have breakfast. The general manager called in three other managers, and our meeting began. I needed them to tell me everything about Jacky's input in the business.

I got out my notebook and pen and was all ears! The employees loved Jacky. A lot had changed since she joined. For some reason, the sales had gone up, people worked beyond 5p.m., and the green pastures out there had seemingly faded away since the employees stopped leaving. What was happening? What had Jacky done? Was she the missing link at Wanjihia Light Company Limited? What followed was two hours of interaction every morning for two weeks.

Mr. Wanjihia eventually appreciated having his daughter on board. This gave him time to venture into a new business idea. He had always dreamt of doing business with his former classmates; there was no better business than quarry stones for their rental housing venture. He was happy to get some money out of his friends' pockets as they bought building stones for their multiple construction projects.

While Wanjihia was away, Jacky did a few things differently. She was at work by 6.00a.m. every day. Interestingly, the employees started reporting to work at 6.00a.m. too. She decided to get everyone tea, cookies, and some fruit, assuming they hadn't had breakfast by then. Every morning was graced with an informal chit-chat in the common room on what they intended to achieve that day. By noon Jacky realised that she needed a nap. She would then lock her office door and sleep for thirty minutes. This explained the large duvet on her couch. She turned one of the open offices into a resting room where anyone who needed to refresh could take a power nap. To get to the office at 6.00a.m. through the usual traffic jam, some employees had to wake up at 4.00a.m. By noon, they had already put in six hours of hard work. They were surely exhausted; the nap room was a welcome addition.

This was different from the masculine rebuke they received any time Wanjihia found an employee seeming to laze around or looking sleepy. The employees felt loved. They were indebted to Jacky, and the only way to express their love was to ensure sales increased. They knew that increased sales would keep Wanjihia away, assured that all was well. The sales and the profits took an upward trend. Jacky decided to share the success with the employees. She offered a reward of three percent of the profits from increased sales every month. If the profits grew from two million in January to 2.1 million shillings in February, they would get three percent of the extra 100,000 shillings as a bonus. If the profits in March were 2.3 million shillings, they would get three percent of 200,000 shillings as a bonus. This was divided equally among the employees. They called it Jacky's Success Sharing scheme (J.S.S.S.), and it became a regular topic of the informal chit-chat in the morning over breakfast. The team was determined to push the sales up every month. And push they did. Wanjihia benefited from the JSS scheme too. He was excited to see some extra coins in his salary account.

> *The employees felt loved, and Jackie shared the success with them.*

One morning during the usual chit-chat, Triza, an employee in the accounts department, asked Jacky if they could incorporate solar panels into their product line. This was a brilliant idea. Jacky had no idea where to start, so she requested Triza to research and run the solar project. Upon implementation, the new product line became a success story. It increased the company's revenue more than any other product. This was an additional revenue stream. Jacky introduced a second reward, Triza's Ingenuity Scheme (TIS). Any new successful product line would be rewarded with a company car, fully maintained and fueled by the company. It was everyone's dream to drive.

> *It was paramount to take risks in the ever-changing business world. Testing new products was a worthwhile risk.*

Jacky had realised that it was paramount to take risks to survive in the ever-changing business world. Testing new products was a worthwhile risk. I was curious to know if there was anything about Jacky's leadership that they were unhappy with. I had to promise to be tight-lipped about it. Jacky's over-trusting attitude had left the company in debt when one of the employees, Dave, thought of an additional product, clay heaters, that were meant to keep houses warm. It was an excellent way to diversify, but she should have done some due diligence before committing the company to a huge capital and operational cost loan. She should have also involved the rest of the team. Instead, it was left to Dave to deal with alone. There was no maker-checker. Dave bought substandard machines, which all broke down within a month. He had also sourced poor-quality raw materials. He might have selfishly pocketed some funds, hence his dishonesty over the quality of the machine and raw materials. The whole project ended up as a total mess and a huge loss. Wanjihia almost fired his daughter at this point. Her greatest weakness was that she needed things to move and move fast. At times, the speed came with poorly thought-out business ideas and losses. However, the ventures that worked brought a lot of growth and progress.

> *There was a need to create a balance between friendship and work.*

One manager said Jacky favoured girls in her age bracket over the others. There was a need to create a balance between friendship and work. The favourites would lord it over the rest of the team, making it difficult for managers to keep them accountable. They had a way of pushing Jacky to cover up their mistakes. Besides that, in their opinion, Jacky was a better leader than her dad in growing the business and handling staff. The employees requested that I keep this exclusive information a secret.

I met Wanjihia and his wife for dinner one evening. They were happy to have let Jacky take the lead at work but agreed that they needed to go through her ideas before she implemented them. I realised that the couple needed this talk. I later learnt from Njeri that it was therapeutic since they had argued a lot when the clay heater project that Jacky had initiated sunk millions of shillings. Njeri blamed Wanjihia for spending too much time at the quarry and leaving Jacky to make all the decisions by herself. Wanjihia, on the other hand, blamed Njeri since she was the one who insisted that Jacky should join the company. Wanjihia had other plans for her - she was meant to go for further studies abroad. I was happy to have unknowingly intervened. I felt like a marriage and family therapist.

We agreed on a few things - that Jacky and her parents would hold weekly meetings to bring the other two core family members up to speed with the week's operations. They would also set the tone for the following week. We also agreed that the three would meet with all the managers at the beginning of every month to set targets and introduce any novel ideas as a team. I requested that the two encourage the shy young girl to become bold by appreciating her for work well done. I also challenged them to push her to attend public speaking classes. This would help her take the lead in building collaborations with other businesses where necessary.

As I sat on the balcony of my house one evening, watching the stars, all that filled my mind was the meetings I'd held with Jacky, Njeri, Wanjihia, and their employees. The two weeks at Wanjihia's company were well spent. It was exciting to see the extent to which a daughter had pushed a business into profitability. However, I needed to figure out if there was a common denominator that propelled growth when women took leadership positions. I needed to visit a few more family businesses. I had a few appointments lined up for the next few weeks.

becky joins manufacturing at zeep pharmaceuticals

I scheduled to visit a medicine manufacturing firm for the next two weeks. I had toured the firm when Jose started it about ten years ago, but a lot had changed. At the time, he had two employees, Balozi and Kaura, and one product line - an antacid. His office doubled up as the manufacturing space. This time, I found that they had acquired more land, constructed more manufacturing halls, added twenty more product lines, and gotten more employees. My jaw dropped. What a turnaround! In just ten years, a small pharmaceutical startup that manufactured only one type of medicine had grown into an enterprise that prided itself on transactions worth millions of dollars.

What a transformation! Their positive results were evident. And they were more than just results; they were amazingly massive results! This was extraordinary. I had brought some bananas for Becky, a longtime friend who had joined her husband five years back to support him in running the manufacturing firm. She complained that I had maintained my petite body and was jealous since she had put on quite some weight. We had some catching up to do as we ate the bananas. She took me to her beautiful office. I was curious to know why and how so much had changed in ten years. The last time I visited, Becky worked for a state corporation while her husband's business was struggling, and I needed to hear the details of the change process. She suggested involving the departmental heads to get a more objective view. From my previous experience with Jacky's team, I couldn't agree more that the employees would greatly benefit my research. At some point, the busy Becky requested to sneak out and virtually attend to a prospective customer abroad.

The team of sixteen departmental heads comprised the head of finance, procurement, marketing, customer service, human resource, international sales, and heads of all the twenty different product lines, each handling two. Each product line manufactured a different type of drug or farm input. We agreed to have separate meetings with each of them over the next sixteen days. 'This was going to be adventurous,' I thought to myself. I was looking forward to unearthing the reason for the tremendous success and finding out if it had anything to do with Becky joining the firm. I was already creating an opinion from the results of Wanjihia Light Company Limited, but I had to hold my peace and remain objective instead of making early conclusions.

It was a busy sixteen days of interacting with the Heads of Department (HODs). My contact with each provided enough content for an entire book. The HODs were male and female, aged between 29 – 49 years. Some were graduates from the university, with Zeep being their first employer. Others had previously been employed elsewhere, while others joined the firm immediately after high school, meaning they had learnt all they knew while on the job. Becky later confided in me that their best HOD, Balozi, did not even complete high school. He had learnt everything on the job and brought the best results to the table. His team was always ranked the best in performance and ingenuity. This was an interesting twist from the belief that we must hire the right people from a pool of well-trained candidates for the job to succeed as a business. However, I would not wish to create a hypothesis out of it.

It was unlikely that the HOD Human Resource Management would have hired Balozi. Jose had employed him in the second week after starting the company. There was no interview conducted. Jose only needed someone to assist him with packaging and loading, a task Balozi did very well. Jose and Balozi had since walked a ten-year journey together. Balozi had learnt a lot from Jose, and it was interesting to learn from the other HODs that he had acquired Jose's worldview on almost every matter. Other HODs would fill him in before forwarding any issue to their boss, Jose. They would then amend as necessary from Balozi's feedback and then forward the matter to Jose. They called him the super HOD. In my view, Balozi was Jose's master's degree graduate, even without a high school certificate.

 The super HOD was a tall, dark, and slender man. His long dark afro hair reminded me of musicians of the 80s. I learnt from him how the company operated before and after Becky's arrival from the state corporation. "We were all skeptical when madam joined us," Mr. Super HOD said as he gazed at the roof of his office. At some point, I had to look to determine if a *mwakenya* (reference book) was up there. But it was his style of visualizing the past as he narrated the turn of events one after another. There was a myth that things went from bad to worse when women were on board. The team thought that Becky would be irrational and aggressive. They had been so comfortable working with Jose that they feared Becky would be an unwelcome intrusion.

To their surprise, Becky was a motherly employer who cared about every employee's welfare, ranging from finding out what classes their children were in to how they performed, where their spouses worked, what their ambitions were, where they lived, and so much more. She did not just find out for the sake of it too, but to improve every aspect that mattered to the employees. She paid fees for some dependants, paid hospital bills for sick relatives, visited and helped some to construct family houses, employed some spouses, and encouraged some to take additional courses and further their studies. Her good deeds were endless. All the 16 HODs had positive things to say about Becky's good deeds. One of them called her an angel. Having known Becky for several years, I knew they were right. Becky made the employees feel like the business belonged to all of them.

> *Becky was a motherly employer who cared about every employee's welfare.*

The super HOD mentioned that things had changed since when they were just three in the business, during its inception, back then, they would go for up to two months without salaries. They would do various tasks in the course of a day, making it difficult to specialize and perfect one thing. They were all, including Jose, jacks-of-all-trades. The first person to report to work would clean the office and start packing the drugs manufactured the previous night. Becky injected additional capital to boost the business. "She must have been paid a lot of money as a retirement package from the state corporation," said Mr. Super HOD. He was quite a sanguine and was not shy to speak his mind.

Becky had brought order; she allowed them to specialize in specific areas of operation and encouraged everyone to consider quality a priority. She made them believe their job was not to manufacture drugs but to elongate patients' lives. This made everyone feel like they had a sacred calling to work in partnership with God to improve people's lives.

> *Becky had brought order. She allowed them to specialize in specific areas. Also, she was always willing to learn.*

A unique aspect brought out by one of the HODs was Becky's ability to appreciate that she did not know it all. She was always willing to learn all the manufacturing tips and appreciated the HODs' specialized knowledge. It was their joy to train her step by step. They said she was the humblest human being they had ever met. She assured them that their decisions and actions mattered since they were the subject matter experts. She inspired confidence in them.

Becky gave annual bonuses to the best-performing departments. This created a sense of positive interdepartmental competition. The departmental heads were all involved in setting specific, measurable, and appropriate goals. It was on this basis that their departments would be rewarded. Becky had transformed the team into inspired, motivated, confident, and performing employees.

One of the HODs mentioned that Becky had slowed Jose's speed of doing things. As it was, Jose quickly implemented strategies that were not well thought through. On many occasions, they held meetings whose resolutions would be changed overnight, necessitating urgent impromptu meetings the following morning. Strategies were implemented on the go, and this was exhausting for the employees. Becky had brought some sense of 'let's plan first and then move, and move with speed'. She always used the analogy, better spend the whole day sharpening an axe and take one hour to cut down a tree instead of spending ten hours cutting down a tree using a blunt axe.

> *Better spend the whole day sharpening an axe and take one hour to cut down a tree instead of spending ten hours cutting down a tree using a blunt axe.*

The marketing HOD said that Becky had enriched the firm with new markets from the Ministries of Health and Agriculture. Her engagement with a state corporation previously had given her many networks, which she utilized to grow their market share. Since quality was her main domain, the firm's products always passed the quality test, giving them an upper hand when bidding for government tenders.

I requested the HODs to confide in me if there was anything that Becky needed to improve. Thirteen HODs felt that Becky was a perfect superwoman. Three, however, mentioned that she needed to be more professional when handling staff problems. They thought that some staff members were taking advantage of her generosity. She would give them money without due diligence, and some were giving false information, for example, lying about the death of a parent. Dishonest employees knew how to extort finances from her. My responsibility as Becky's friend was to figure out how to encourage her to have a welfare committee that would vet arising issues that required her help.

I was keen to find out who was behind the twenty product lines. This was quite a mouthful within ten years. Becky explained later that she encouraged Jose to travel along with the different Heads of Department on his trips abroad. This way, they would all come home with great ideas, which Jose modified for viability. This was how new products were born. Everyone who came up with an idea was encouraged to run with it. It was interesting to note that the HODs molded each new product line from scratch, and Jose only intervened to ensure the product was a locally viable business.

Some products were born out of knowledge and product transfer from new employees who came on board from competing firms. Such products became viable immediately since the competitors had already done market research and sensitization. Other products were discoveries of the company laboratory team. It was amazing to see what humans could achieve, pushing beyond existing limits.

By this time, I had realised that it was the combination of Jose's astute business timing and Becky's social intelligence and professionalism that brought about the incredible growth. I believe Jose and Becky were transformational leaders.

The month went down with loads of lessons from two family businesses, both of which had been started by the men. One had a daughter, and the other a wife on board. There seemed to be immense growth in the businesses after the ladies joined. I returned to the library to research whether transformational leadership directly impacted business growth and performance. From the literature, it did, indeed. Would the two businesses have grown to their current extent if the two ladies had not come on board? I don't know for sure, but I think the answer is no. The high turnover of employees prior to the ladies' arrival was an undeniable testament.

Professor Dennis Tourish wrote a worthwhile book, *The Dark Side of Transformational Leadership*. He opined that followers, led by transformational leaders, tended to over-rely on their leaders' views because of assuming that the leader was always right and better equipped than the followers to decide the best approach towards issues. This could be true to some extent, but from my experience with the two family businesses, the ladies on board might have neutralized overreliance on leadership by giving their employees the flexibility to make decisions.

Weeks three and four were a success. I looked forward to week five and to a new engagement. This was getting more exciting than I expected.

emmah, the iron lady
at ham group of schools

I knew weeks five and six would be challenging times of research. I visited a school that belonged to Emmah, the lady who topped my class every time in primary school. I remember, once in class three, wishing she would lead a school one day when we grew up. This child's wish had come true. I should have wished for presidency - maybe it too would have come true. I received a rapturous reception; it was an emotional reunion after more than thirty years.

We went for lunch at a nearby hotel, ate fish, and joked about how we needed the omega-3 from the fish to keep our brains lubricated since age was catching up with us. We had a lot to discuss. We leaped from topic to topic, like newly born calves; our primary school head teacher, the late Mr. Kiguru, who had influenced our lives positively, and our class prefect, who ended up miserable after engaging in drugs. Our stories ranged from childhood to college to adulthood, not in any specific order, but back and

forth I nearly forgot my mission.

Emmah had studied Early Childhood Education at the university. She loved children and decided, at some point, to leave formal employment and try building her own school from scratch. It was not an easy task. She didn't have enough finances, and no bank was willing to gamble on her startup and provide capital. More so, no bank would risk trusting a woman's business idea. However, she managed to hire a room as an initial class that attracted ten children by the end of the first term. By the end of the first year, she had two classes, each with fifteen children, and an extra teacher to handle one class while she took the other. Five years into the business, she had acquired a piece of land and put up a few structures. The school population had grown to four hundred pupils with ten teachers. This was tremendous growth.

Emmah turned downcast at this point. I would have expected her to keep smiling since things were looking up. She had acquired her own premises and had a growing population of students, which translated into a growing business. I was startled when she began to cry. I got confused. Emmah regained composure and explained that her husband, Ric, was retrenched from work at the end of the fifth year of the school. Therefore, she welcomed him to the business and looked forward to an upward growth spiral. Ric had been a supervisor in a five-star hotel in the city for over ten years, a job he loved.

Emmah received him with an open heart, made him an additional signatory to all the school bank accounts, and requested him to take the lead. She was practicing what her pastor taught her in church. The man is the head of the house. She imagined this would apply to her business, too, now that Ric was home. The future looked bright. She had an additional pair of hands, or so she thought.

Two months after Ric's arrival, Jane, Emmah's best teacher and first employee, brought in her resignation letter. Emmah was in shock. She hadn't seen this coming but acknowledged receipt of the letter and painfully let her go. By the third month, she had received more than five other resignation letters. Now, this was alarming. Her world was crumbling down. She knew something wasn't right. She gathered courage, invited one of the teachers to her office, and asked what the challenge was. It turned out the teachers had not been paid in months! She had left all the financial duties, including collecting fees, ensuring funds were banked, and paying suppliers and teachers to Ric.

Emmah's instincts made her call the banks immediately to find out her account balances. By this time, my mouth was agape, and my ears itched to find to find out what was next. There were substantial overdrafts in all five bank accounts. She told me that she fainted and only regained consciousness in a hospital bed. Loss of five teachers translated to parents transferring their children to neighbouring schools. Word had gone round that all the teachers wanted to leave. Emmah was crushed to see the business she had spent so much time and energy building over the years tumbling down in months. She blamed herself for allowing Ric to come on board. Her marriage had been struggling too.

I later learnt that Emmah had gathered the courage to start a new school in a different district. She left her initial business to Ric, who ran it down, and the banks auctioned off the premises. The new school grew to accommodate a kindergarten, primary and secondary school, and plans were underway to construct a college. Hers was a sought-after brand. It was prestigious for parents to take their children to Ham Group of Schools. Emmah, the school director, introduced me to the principals of the primary and secondary schools, who later introduced me to the kindergarten's senior teacher. I looked forward to the following day. I was certain that the staff team had many lessons for me. I needed to find out if any of the teachers from the former school had joined the new one. I couldn't sleep that night. The thought of Ric messing up Emmah's years of hard work was too disturbing.

I woke up early and drove to Ham Group of Schools (HGS). The two principals, the senior kindergarten teacher, and I entered a well-furnished office with a taste of class, a hallmark of Emmah's taste. I was all ears as I listened to their narration of the journey to building a brand. The senior kindergarten teacher, Madam Liz, had joined Emmah while at the former school. She shed tears as she remembered how they had to start all over to build HGS. They initially went for months without full salaries since their income could not match the expenditure. The school began with ten pupils,

> *Emmah was very hard-working and always led by example. Everyone felt a sense of personal growth, a sense of progress.*

but they believed in Emmah's vision. She had done it before, and they were sure she would do it again. This conviction kept them on board. In one year, the school's population had grown to a level that could sustain operations. Ham Kindergarten was starting to take shape.

Madam Liz said that Emmah was very hard-working and always led by example. She also ensured that all her teachers attended every educational seminar that would benefit them and the school. Everyone felt a sense of personal growth, a sense of progress. There was a very low staff turnover rate. Separation mostly happened when one was moving to join the Teachers Service Commission, a government body, which was a rare occurrence.

Madam Liz said that Emmah had a way with the parents. It was as if she spoke straight to their hearts. She knew almost all of them by name and would visit any child who fell sick or was admitted to the hospital. The parents loved her. The children enjoyed celebrating birthdays at school. Emmah had a birthday cake from a nearby bakery delivered to her office every morning during the term. The birthday babies of the day would then line up in her office for a birthday song and cut the cake, which would then be shared among the pupils and members of staff. Everyone was made to feel special. Word went around that this was the best school in the district. The children were the greatest ambassadors and marketers. They spoke about their good school every time they got an opportunity, in church, to their neighbours and relatives. Consequently, the enrollment went up. "Within no time, there was a need to start a primary, secondary, and, recently, a college section," Madam Liz said as her eyes lit up in fulfilment. I asked her if they had experienced any near misses. I needed to get any dark sides without looking like I was probing for Emmah's weaknesses.

> *Everyone was made to feel special.*

After a heavy sigh, Liz mentioned that she sometimes felt like too many things were happening simultaneously. She also felt they needed to think through strategies before implementing them. They implemented and readjusted on the go. Liz indicated that this could be quite confusing. This triggered a memory in my head. It reminded me of Jose, Becky's husband at Zeep Pharmaceuticals, who would execute, make changes, and re-change on the go.

One such case was when Emmah put up an expensive building to hold a commercial cafeteria. The idea was to get an extra revenue stream to supplement the school fees. It so happened that she also constructed a library block next to the cafeteria. The two buildings were ready for use at the same time. The management team recruited chefs and waitresses for the cafeteria and librarians for the library.

> *She felt they needed to think through strategies before implementing them.*

After a successful recruitment process, the two ventures went into operation. However, the cafeteria, which was open to the public, disturbed the necessary quiet of a library environment. There was constant conflict between the librarians and the waiters. But was it really their fault? Or was the challenge the speedy execution of ideas that were barely thought through? Separate locations for the two worthwhile projects should have been considered. The cafeteria had to be converted to a different use at some point. Some expensive readjustments were made, and it was turned into classrooms. Liz felt they would have averted some challenges had they taken up one project at a time. The principals nodded in agreement, and I could tell the feeling was mutual.

The two principals were free to manage the primary and high schools as they willed. Emmah did not micromanage them. She believed that whatever decisions they made would be the best. This was motivating but also challenging because they had to do everything right the first time. They felt a shared responsibility for the schools' success. They were at liberty to adapt to changes in the education system and bring in new techniques where necessary. This was liberating. They both went out of their way to make the schools better. The principals' sense of ownership and responsibility trickled down to their staff. It was a whole team of motivated staff. Waking up to go to work was an adventure.

I visited the school during the worldwide pandemic - COVID-19. Schools had been shut down, and physical interactions had been banned. The teachers, out of their own volition, created dynamic learning experiences for children to learn virtually using electronic devices. The pupils who did not have gadgets for one reason or the other, were allowed to borrow from the school. This sense of considering the well-being of every pupil was unmatched. I spent an hour every evening with the team. My notebook was full, and two weeks had elapsed. I had learnt a lot.

I held a meeting with Emmah on the last day. We stayed in her office until midnight. We did not realise that time had gone by so fast. She had earlier requested me to give her any feedback that would be helpful from my interactions within the organization. I explained to her the impact of having too many projects coming up simultaneously. She hadn't realised that her zeal to see things moving and changing fast caused stress on the employees. She resolved to form a committee to help think through all her grand strategies and fine-tune them before implementation.

I was keen to hear what her next plan was. She was indeed an iron lady. Emmah dreamt of franchising Ham Group of Schools one day. This meant having a "Ham School" in every district. Ham was already a huge brand, with its success story published severally on national media outlets. I offered to assist her with this great venture. But my advice was that she works on franchising the kindergarten first. We wrote a to-do list. My duties were to get a lawyer to work out a franchise agreement and also assist in protecting the business's intellectual property. The teachers at the kindergarten were to compile an operational manual for franchisees. Emmah's task was to schedule meetings every evening with prospective franchisees from every district. The school accountant was tasked with setting up the royalties and other fees that would be required from the franchisees.

After interacting with the three organizations, Wanjihia's, Zeep, and HGS, I could roughly paint a picture of the attributes that brought about success in institutions led by women. The issues that required improvement by the women in leadership were also getting clearer.

the girls' dinner

I was back to my balcony, scanning through my notebook looking through the details of the three organizations I had visited over the last six weeks. I still had some loose ends to tie up, and I thought to bring the three ladies, Jacky, Becky, and Emmah, together for dinner. This would be the panacea, an answer to all my questions. I was sure my curiosity would then be quenched. I needed to conclude my quest to find out how women performed when allowed to lead family businesses. I made phone calls to the three, and they were all available the following evening. Their acceptance was an honour as the trio was a very busy lot.

Saitoti, an old-time friend and primary school classmate, owns the Ole Lenala Hotel in Nairobi. I often visited this serene place when I needed to relax or write. I dropped the three ladies the location pin to Saitoti's place and looked forward to our date. I was a bit nervous and unsure how to go about getting the three strangers to bond. But I was almost sure Becky, the sanguine, would do her thing and quickly sort this out for me. The dress code was red and black. This was meant to help break the ice.

I sat at a gazebo next to a live band with very soft country music, a great environment to complete reading *When Breath Becomes Air* by Paul Kalanithi, a book I had put aside to complete the busy interviews at the three family businesses.

Njeri was the first to arrive at 7 p.m. sharp. I did not expect her; I expected her daughter, Jacky. She was dressed in a long, warm, black dress. Her red belt and red doll shoes met the black and red dress code. She looked fresh and ready for dinner. She loved the place at first sight, and I knew I had enlisted a new customer for Saitoti. They had a great team-building place that would be ideal for Wanjihia Lighting Company employees.

I was glad to hear Njeri confess that the weekly meetings I had suggested for the trio, Wanjihia, Jacky, and Njeri, were continuing and bearing fruits. They also met the HODs monthly as agreed to set targets and chart the way forward. She acknowledged that this had been very helpful.

No sooner had we exchanged pleasantries than Emmah walked in. It was 7.05p.m. She looked sharp in a red jumpsuit, a black fascinator on her hair, a black belt, and black heels. The heels were several inches high to complement her short stature. I introduced her to Njeri, and they instantly kicked off a conversation. I was glad the bonding had started. I excused myself and dashed to the washroom. On my way back, I met Becky at the entrance. It was exciting to see her. She was dressed in a black skirt suit and red heels. Her small red handbag completed the great look. It was 7.10p.m. The dinner invitation was for 7.30p.m., but all the ladies had arrived early. Becky and I walked toward Emmah and Njeri, who were already in an intense conversation. Becky introduced herself, and the three ladies bonded effortlessly. Different topics came up. The first was the dress code, then the luxurious hotel, then husbands, then children. I realised we needed to serve dinner, or the stories would never end. It was interesting to note that these were real women with normal women stories. The one remarkable thing was that they led multimillion-shilling businesses. For sure, young Jacky was wise to have sent her mother, Njeri. She would have felt awkward with these older women, aged between forty and fifty-two. Their stories would not have made much sense to her.

It was dinner time, and as usual, Saitoti never disappoints. I texted him and invited him to come and meet my friends. The tall, well-built, good-looking man in his late forties spoke the Queen's English. Our English teacher, who was also the school headmaster, the late Mr. Kiguru, had taught us well. Our school was located in the depths of a village, where the English language was taught in our mother tongue. It was only by God's grace that we could speak fluent English. As a professional businessman, he gave the ladies his business card and requested for theirs. He informed them about all the good things the hotel offered, including catering for staff meals for various organizations. He nearly took over my meeting. They had too many questions for him, especially Emmah, who was considering catering as one of the courses to offer in her upcoming college. This would be a great place for her students to practice during their internships. I realised that the women saw every new acquaintance as a possible business link.

I whispered to Emmah that Saitoti was still single and would be a good match for her. She was divorced and lonely. Thirty years back, we had teased each other while in primary school about which boy liked whom. This felt like a

> *The women saw every new acquaintance as a possible business link.*

continuation of the teasing. The iron lady gave me a nod and said she liked him too and that he looked familiar, but then added that she was too busy for relationships at the time. Her focus was on starting and growing her dream college, and getting the franchising business off its feet. I admitted that I was joking and told her that Saitoti was married. I was surprised neither could figure out where they had met before - we had all been classmates in primary school. I chose not to remind either of them at this point.

Dinner was great. Served as a buffet, we had chapati, mashed potatoes, fish, chicken, vegetables, Swahili pilau, and ice cream, assorted fresh juices, and fruits for dessert. I realised I needed to take charge of the conversation lest I failed to obtain what I needed. It was nothing formal, but I required everyone to tell their story as family business leaders.

After dinner, I requested Saitoti to join us so that I could also get a man's perspective. It was worthwhile. "Do you think women are the reason family businesses scale up?" I asked.

> *Women have the ability to build something from nothing and grow it into a great venture. They nurture, encourage and develop by nature.*

Emmah went first, sharing her point of view that women have the ability to build something from nothing and grow it into a great venture. They nurture by nature, encourage by nature, and develop others by nature. She gave an example of a small child. From a crawling baby, a mother encourages a child to make their first step. The mother knows when to encourage a second and third step, depending on the child's ability. Within no time, the child will be up walking and then running. This feminine instinct is not only in humans but in animals too. This inborn trait in women nurtures and grows businesses, employees, and customers' portfolios. Emmah was a teacher with early childhood training, so this great analogy made a lot of sense. We were all ears.

Emmah paused, and Saitoti broke the silence respectfully. He mentioned that women had more patience to nurture growth in business ventures one step at a time. Patience is a natural trait needed when bringing up children, as Emmah had mentioned earlier. He couldn't agree more. I quickly took advantage and asked if this differed from how men operated. According to Saitoti, men naturally start businesses but need someone to nurture and grow them, and then they will go out and start another venture or bring in another product and expand the business.

> *They have more patience to nurture growth in business ventures one step at a time.*

A business needs the starting energy, where men seemingly do well. A business also needs the nurturing energy, and women tend to excel in this. Both men and women can handle business development, which entails bringing in new products or business ideas. The cycle continues with the women nurturing the new products and business ideas. In the animal kingdom, the lion causes conception while the lioness gives birth. She hunts and ensures that her cubs are well-fed. Females own the pride. Males leave the pride at two or three years of age and conquer a new pride. The lion plants a seed, and again, conception happens. The cycle continues. The female species are nurturing by nature, both among animals and human beings.

This analogy got me thinking. I had a lot to write. Flashbacks of how Jacky, the young university graduate, disrupted her father's business by providing care and nurture to employees ran through my mind. The breakfast and naps she provided scaled up the business to unimaginable levels. Becky and her manufacturing business also came to mind. She was involved in her employees' lives. She paid fees and hospital bills for their dependents. She even assisted some in constructing their dream homes. This was nurture. No wonder her employees called her an angel. No wonder her employees felt like they were a part of the family business and worked hard to ensure it succeeded. Emmah, the iron lady, ensured her teachers attended as many educational seminars as possible. She invested in their improvement. Her daily birthday cakes for anyone within the school fraternity celebrating their birthdays were a selfless act of love and care for people at an individual level. This must have created wonderful childhood memories for the children. I got so engrossed in the flashback that I almost disappeared into my own world. I was distracted by Saitoti's deep voice when he signaled a waitress to serve us tea. I did not want to embarrass myself by asking what they were discussing while I was lost in my thoughts. I was the host and was expected to be fully attentive.

As we sipped our tea, Njeri told her story of how their business became successful when their daughter, Jacky, joined her dad. Young as she was, she was able to lead by example; and reporting to the office early challenged the employees to do the same. Hence, so much was achieved by mid-day each day. The nap room was full of sleepy heads every noon. They were free to sleep as long as they wished, yet, everyone was up in less than an hour, ready for the afternoon's work. The employees got free breakfast every morning, which made them feel appreciated. My sanguine friend, Becky, suggested that Njeri hooks up her daughter with Jacky so that similar magic would happen at Zeep too.

I was happy that Saitoti felt comfortable with the ladies. He applauded Njeri for encouraging her daughter to join her dad at an early age. This would give her time to make mistakes and learn from her elders early enough. He said she would be a great strategic leader by the time she hit her second anniversary at work and would move the business to unbelievable heights. This was because the younger generation embraced technology, thus enhancing unprecedented growth and sustainability beyond borders.

Emmah had been quiet all along, and this bothered me a bit. I later learnt that she had scheduled a webinar with her teachers that night and needed to leave. She excused herself, pulled out her laptop, and moved to a corner. She was back in half an hour. She hoped she had not missed too much. I was still surprised that Emmah and Saitoti had not recognised each other. Their recollection of faces seen in the past was undoubtedly poor.

Becky had already shared her input while Emmah was away. She humbly admitted that joining her husband, Jose, at the factory had resulted in an instant upward spiral of profit. The business had scaled up wholesomely. She attributed this to the fact that she was concerned about every employee as an individual. If a mother gave birth to fifteen children, she would know them by name, understand everyone's unique character, meet each of their personal needs, and encourage every individual to exceed their limits.

Becky's analogy was mind-boggling. I remembered reading somewhere that one characteristic of transformational leaders was the giving of individual attention. I wouldn't have understood it better. I recalled my conversation with her Heads of Department, who described her as an angel. She knew their children, parents, and siblings and even attended their family functions. No wonder they felt like they owned the company too. The employees felt like family.

It was getting late, and we needed to go home and rest well enough to attend to our diverse duties of building the nation the following day. I was glad that this meeting was successful. My notebook was now filled up. I requested the ladies to allow me to buy lunch for their Heads of Department at an appropriate time at Saitoti's place. I had a great plan ahead. There was no objection whatsoever.

Saitoti beckoned me as we headed for the door. He invited me to join him and his wife for dinner the following evening. I was sure he was up to something. I could tell he had enjoyed our discussion and was happy we had made him a part of it. I signaled Emmah, just a few steps ahead, to slow down. She walked back, and I made the two go down memory lane slowly but surely. They were both shocked when they realised how long it had taken them to recognise each other. Emmah made fun of Saitoti's old self, a short, dark, and slender boy with no signs of ever growing tall, now well-built and handsome. No wonder he didn't ring a bell. I could see the excitement as they hugged, laughed, and shed tears simultaneously. We immediately planned for our class three reunion at Saitoti's place in a month's time. Emmah was gracious enough to organize this reunion.

In a few minutes, I was home, exhausted but fulfilled. Some building blocks were falling into place. My curiosity was slowly but surely getting quenched. I couldn't sleep from the different thoughts buzzing through my mind that night. It dawned on me that the businesses I had visited were in the first generation, apart from Wanjihia Light Company Limited, which had Jacky, making it a second-generation interaction. I looked forward to visiting a multigenerational family venture. A third and fourth generation would be such an adventure for me.

back-to-back meetings
at ole lenala

Someone must have forwarded my clock the following day. It was evening already. I grabbed my yellow dress and warm black jacket and left for Ole Lenala. I loved this place. It gave me memories of our days upcountry when growing up. We would sit and listen to the trees rustling, the birds singing, the waters trickling, and the wind whistling. It was nature at its best, a place full of tranquility. I sat at my usual spot.

Saitoti walked towards me, wearing a broad smile. A beautiful tall, dark, slender lady with a glow on her face walked behind him. "This must be your pretty wife," I said. Saitoti introduced her as Omy. Her broad smile, accompanied by dimples on her cheeks, warmed the atmosphere. I immediately liked her affable personality. He introduced me as his primary school classmate who was doing some research on family businesses. Omy highlighted that she would be happy to host me since there was a lot to discuss about their family business, "The Ole Lenala."

I could tell that Saitoti was a little nervous. The confident gentleman that I knew seemed to have faded overnight. Or was he angry? I couldn't quite tell, but something was amiss.

Saitoti opened up and explained that he had invited me because Omy had been away from the hotel business for three months following a conflict between them. This caught me by surprise. I was neither a marriage counsellor nor an arbitrator. Why would Saitoti call on me in such a situation? What a way to meet his wife for the first time! I did not know where to focus my eyes. It felt awkward. He went on to state that he had mentioned to Omy that I had met quite a number of women who had taken up leadership in family businesses. He said that Omy and he wanted to learn a few things about operating efficiently. I was still a little confused. Saitoti had met the three ladies the previous night. Why didn't he explain to Omy what he gathered from them instead of bringing me on board?

Omy calmly interrupted my thoughts. "It is sad that we have to meet you at a time when our relationship is on the rocks, but this meeting may be what we need right now. Saitoti keeps saying I am overly generous and behave like an ice cream seller, seeking to be loved by all the hotel workers. His comment hurts a lot because I wake up early and work long hours. "I give the business my all," she lamented. By this time, her tears were flowing freely. Saitoti felt that Omy was over-concerned with their employees' personal lives and gave too much money away. This affected their finances and drained their working capital kitty.

The hotel would shut down in about two months if they did nothing. Saitoti was not going to watch this happen. Hence, sending Omy home was the best option, in his opinion. With this background, there was definitely work to be done. Becky came to mind. She is also a generous girl. Her employees call her an angel. Did Becky have limits? If she did, could Omy borrow some tips from her? I quickly called Becky and requested her to join us on her way home. I told her I was with a mentee who needed her expertise and wisdom to stay afloat. Otherwise, they were sinking.

Becky never disappoints; she was with us within an hour. Her plus-size body was dressed in a black free dress and yellow sandals. What a coincidence! We were both in yellow and black, and Becky was quick to point this out immediately upon joining us. She greeted Omy with a peculiarly warm hug and called her by name. Saitoti and I glanced at each other in shock. Becky and Omy were from the same village and had attended the same primary school. Omy was, however, five classes behind Becky. When Omy joined high school in form one, Becky was in form six in the same national school. No wonder their command of the Queen's language was top-notch. It had been nearly three decades since they last saw each other.

My work here was done. With Becky on board, Omy would be sorted. I signaled Saitoti and we agreed to give Becky and Omy space. Saitoti teased them, saying that they could talk until they developed a business partnership, 'Be & Omy Limited,' short for Becky and Omy.

I immediately excused myself to meet a Nigerian friend who needed to meet me since, as he had indicated, he had a great business idea. I had nicknamed him Oga. We had first met in South Africa during a one-month leadership skills training. The chubby, short and loud Oga arrived dressed in his usual African attire. His laugh was so loud that everyone in the hotel immediately noticed his presence. We walked to the well-manicured garden, where I had reserved a sitting space for two. Oga was hungry, so he ordered some *fufu* and fish. I couldn't have imagined that Nigerian cuisine would be available here. I updated Oga on what I had been up to for the last couple of months as he enjoyed his meal. I mentioned all the lessons I had learnt from the four family businesses I had interacted with, including Saitoti's hotel.

Oga suggested that we do a similar study in Nigeria to find out if the 'women thing,' as he called it, was the same there. It was time to discuss business. He wanted us to meet with his Indian friend, Patel, who ran a food processing plant. Oga was a marketing guru, so I thought he needed to create a marketing strategy for Patel's products. I tried to find out what the deal was in advance, to prepare for the meeting, but Oga was tight-lipped about it. This sounded strange. Oga said he needed me to be very objective about the discussion and explained that my objectivity would be compromised if he told me about it in advance. He received a phone call and put it on speaker mode. From the Indian accent, I could tell it was Patel on the other end. Oga mentioned that he was at Ole Lenala Hotel with a friend. At that point, I saw Omy signal me and knew I needed to check in with them. I did not wait to hear the next part of Patel and Oga's conversation.

Quite eager to listen to Omy and Becky, I quickly excused myself using sign language and dashed inside the hotel. Omy's glowing face was lit up, her dimples deeper, and her tears seemed to have completely dried up. Becky must have had a fruitful conversation with her. Omy thanked me for bringing Becky on board. She had learnt so much.

Becky had shared the process she used to give donations: she would ask the accountant to project a certain percentage of the profits and put it in a donations kitty. She would then donate 80 percent of the amount in the kitty annually. Twenty percent would be left unutilized to act as a cushion if the profit projections were not achieved for whatever reason. This was a calculated move. It was scientific. Omy had learnt a lot. She admitted that she did not involve the accountant when giving donations. She would make unaccounted-for withdrawals when any of her employees were in dire need.

I was keen to know what she would do differently going forward. Omy promised to copy-paste Becky's process. She said donations would be a matter that would be discussed and agreed upon by the accountants and human resource managers. This was fulfilling. I proposed to meet with her

> *Donations would be discussed and agreed upon by the accountants and human resource managers. Ultimately, the employees would reduce their over-reliance on Omy and still have their needs*

employees and introduce a staff savings scheme. This would allow them to take up emergency loans or withdraw a percentage of their savings as needed. Ultimately, the employees would reduce the over-reliance on Omy and still have their needs met. They would be responsible for their own needs instead of piling them on Omy. Becky volunteered to mentor

Omy and walk with her on each step of her business journey. In my view, this meeting had ended well.

It was getting late, and I needed to check on Oga. The garden had become chilly and uncomfortable due to unwelcome mosquito bites. I found him sitting inside the hotel with an Indian gentleman. I guessed it might be Patel. I joined them, eager to know what the deal was all about. Oga introduced Patel saying they had studied together at a university in America many years before. Patel looked familiar; I thought he resembled an actor I had seen in one of the Indian movies translated into my mother tongue, but I was sure I had never met him. Oga introduced me as the friend he had mentioned to him before leaving Nigeria the previous week. He was happy to meet me and requested that I visit him at the factory the following day.

Oga was surely hiding something. But whatever it was, I would only find out the following day. It had been a heavy evening, and I needed some rest. I requested Oga to accompany me to the factory the next day, and he agreed.

a visit to patel's
summer fruits company

While in Nigeria, Oga had seen my phone WhatsApp status requesting referrals to third and fourth-generation family businesses. What a true friend. I later realised that this was why Oga hooked me up with Patel. Patel's family business was in the fourth generation! What a miracle for me! Oga had briefed Patel on what I had been doing. Patel was ready to be vulnerable with a stranger on Oga's account.

The Summer Fruits Company's huge grey gate was opened for Oga and me. The smell of fresh fruits and juice was blown smoothly by the wind right into our noses. The attendant, a physically challenged lady on a wheelchair, offered us a visitors' book in which to record our personal details. This was lesson number one for me. I later learned that she was Patel's aunt. The beauty of family businesses is that they take in family members just as they are. They love them anyway and anyhow. This was impressive.

We were offered seats at the reception and requested to wait for a few minutes for Mr. Patel's assistant. Oga had never been to Patel's family business either. I could tell that he was in shock. The leather seats in the reception area were worth an arm and a leg. It was a huge venture, with throngs of employees dressed in white dust coats, swiftly moving up and down. Some carried cartons, while others carried empty trays.
Some were pushing trolleys while others
carried documents. In a few minutes, a beautiful dark lady in a white dress walked towards us with a smile.

She walked us to Mr. Patel's office and requested that we wait a few minutes as he was inspecting some new machinery. The office was spacious, with a lot of natural light coming in through the huge windows. The furniture looked expensive and classy. One could tell that Mr. Patel had a taste for good things.

We walked on a red carpet right from the door and were offered some assorted fruits and juices as refreshments. This was welcome since the fruity aroma in the air was making me hungry already.

I noticed that Oga, who had been quiet all along, was staring at a picture on the wall. It was unlike him to stay silent. It was a photo of their university classmates in their fourth year. "This brings back a lot of memories," he said, "It was the day before our graduation." Patel walked in just in time to complete Oga's statement. "And we had planned to dance the whole night, but, unfortunately, Oga's music system fell and broke into pieces." He paused. "The intended dance party was ruined," they both said in chorus. Oga's loud voice was back. They hugged and laughed and got into talking. They almost forgot I was there. I had to clear my throat severally to draw back their attention.

Mr. Patel explained that he had gone to inspect a new machine that would pack fruits in cans at ten times the speed of the machine they had been using for the last sixty-three years. He further explained that his great-grandfather had bought the older machine. This was getting exciting. Patel took us to the fruit canning hall. It was a beehive of activity with smooth operations and everything flowed perfectly. At this point, I was wondering if I could request Patel to hand me over to any of the women in leadership as they took their rounds with Oga. But I didn't want to sound rude, so I held my horses. Oga and I were offered gift packs of fruit juices and canned fruits as we walked out of the canning hall. This was special, and I couldn't wait to peep and see what it was. As if Mr. Patel could read my thoughts, he revealed that the package contained pineapple, passion, and mango juices. These were in season. He added that we would find the dragon fruit, pawpaw, and orange juices and fruits the next time we visited.

Patel offered to take me to his wife's office so we could get to know each other. He said she was expecting me. I was glad I didn't have to ask about leaving the guys to accomplish my mission. Namrata was a petite lady dressed in an Indian white and gold saree. She looked beautiful. Her smile was so welcoming. "This must be the lady you talked about last night," she said as she held my hand firmly. "This is her, and she is all yours," Patel responded. Oga and Namrata had met in Nigeria before. She was pleased to meet him again. I came purposely to steal some business tips from your husband, Oga joked loudly. Oga gave Namrata a big hug. She asked about his wife and children. I could tell the two families were very close. Patel joked that he was jealous of Oga's extended hug and pulled him away as they left us to continue our discussions.

Namrata took me around the factory and explained every process, from fruit harvesting to sorting, cleaning, peeling, juicing, or slicing, and canning. She explained that the plant had done this for the last seventy years. Patel's great-grandfather had started the plant. At first, the workers managed the processes manually, until after seven years, when he bought some machines, which Patel had now replaced with modern ones, one by one. "Your husband has done a great job!" I exclaimed. Patel had been a miracle to the plant.

Patel had mentioned that Namrata had a hand in the 60 percent increase in sales since she joined Summer Fruit Company, SFC, as they called it. I asked Namrata what her role was at SFC. She was the deputy chief executive officer. Her main role was ensuring that every section of the firm ran smoothly. She was the oil that lubricated every department. She loved her job, although some days were hectic and draining. Namrata explained that she was at the firm by 8.00 a.m. every day. She then held daily meetings with all the department heads from 8.15 a.m. to 8.35 a.m. to agree on the day's targets and discuss the previous days' operations. The business operated without Heads of Department before Namrata joined SFC.

Namrata's maiden task was to put a structure in place. She ensured that every employee had a job description, targets, and key performance indicators.

Namrata's maiden task was to put a structure in place. Her thoughts were that this structure would ensure a proper flow of command and communication. She also ensured that every employee had a job description, targets, and key performance indicators. This made everyone responsible, both as team members and as individuals. At first, there was some resistance, but she stood her ground. Looking at how professional the operations had become, employees wondered how they initially operated.

We were interrupted by one of the heads of department. There had been an accident in the packaging room; half the packaging cartons were on fire, and none of the fire extinguishers was working. The health and safety team was away on a retreat. Namrata ran towards the packaging bay, and I followed. Everyone looked confused and ran helter-skelter. The packaging room was on the other side of the premises, about 800 meters from Namrata's office. I hadn't gone to the gym for a while and was panting by the time we got there.

I did not see any smoke. Was the fire out already? Namrata's high heels were in her hands. I hadn't realised she ran barefoot. We got to the bay, and all the cartons were intact. "Was it a fire drill?" Namrata asked helplessly, "Yes, Madam," one of the employees responded. "In the event of a fire, all the cartons in the bay would have burned down. Also, next time, Madam, use a car to come this way. It is faster and safer." Namrata had failed the drill test. A group of seven employees dressed in overalls came from an office next to the packing bay. I later learnt this was the Health and Safety Team. There was no retreat. It was part of the drill. Namrata had approved some money a few days previously for them to attend a retreat, but in the real sense, they had been at the firm all along, planning and scheming the drill.

Namrata smiled at them and assured the team she would never fail a fire drill again. It was interesting that her employees would appraise her safety skills and offer genuine below-average feedback without fear. I was feeling drained and exhausted from the sprint. But I had work to do.

Namrata and I got into the health and safety pick-up. The head of the department gave us a lift and dropped us at her office. Her feet were sore. It was hard to believe her employees had made her go through this torture. "I laid the rules and must follow them too," she said. She confided in me that this was her second time failing this test.

I was eager to grab a packet of juice from my gift pack to quench my thirst. Namrata requested that I ask questions to which she would respond. This would make our interaction more structured. I pulled out my green notebook and read out some questions. The first was to find out how she compared the performance of the four generations. She had much respect for the first generation that came up with the business idea. It was an idea that had stood the test of seven decades. She acknowledged that every generation performed its best during its time. I was eager to find out if every generation had a woman in leadership. The first did not, but the second, third, and fourth had women on board. She said that all the women had brought something new. Her mother-in-law, who was in the third generation, introduced the use of technology in most of the operations. Patel's grandmother, who was in the second generation, had initiated alliances and collaborations that would be beneficial many years down the line. Namrata's job was to improve the use of technology and build more alliances since the foundation had already been laid. She structured the operations, introduced job descriptions, and established an employee appraisal system.

Namrata opined that the men looked at the bigger picture and worked towards it. They were not keen on 'how' things were done but on 'what' had to

> *Namrata's job was to improve the use of technology and build more alliances. She believed that women focused on the 'how', which was essential in delivering the 'what'.*

be done. She believed that women focused on the 'how', which was essential in delivering the 'what.' I liked the way she played with words to send a point home. Women provided a competitive advantage by ensuring they hired the right staff and retained them for a long time. Retention was maintained by the 'how.' I interpreted the 'how' to mean culture - how things are done here. I was learning a lot, and I liked it.

We agreed to catch up that evening at Hotel Ole Lenala. Namrata, Patel, and Oga were travelling to Nigeria the following morning, so I suggested we spend some more time together before they left. It had been a busy day. I dashed home to freshen up, ready for our evening meeting. I was very grateful to learn about three great women of different generations from a single organization.

I called Saitoti and requested him to make *fufu* for Oga in advance. I then realised it would be unfair to order Oga's food and leave out Patel and Namrata. I immediately called Oga and asked him what the couple preferred for dinner. *"Fufu!"* He exclaimed. I learnt later that the two love birds and business associates, Patel and Namrata, fought over *fufu* every time they visited Nigeria. Saitoti was excited to make *fufu* for four. I had decided to give it a try too.

Saitoti was at his usual corner, looking calm but very excited. As I walked towards him, I noticed he was smiling, and he quickly grabbed his phone. He was calling his wife, Omy, to join us. I was so glad that she was back to work. 'What a miracle!' I thought. They had daily online meetings with her newly-found mentor, Becky. Saitoti exclaimed that he now had a Chief Operations Officer for the hotel. He was happy with the progress. His wife was now more strategic when making decisions and solving problems. Omy brought me a glass of ice-cold pineapple juice. I wondered how she knew I was dehydrated and needed a cold drink. She was grateful she was learning so much from Becky. She no longer handed out donations from the office kitty. She had talked to her staff about saving some funds monthly for a rainy day. This was going to work wonders.

No sooner had I finished drinking my delicious juice than the trio, Patel, Namrata, and Oga, joined us. Oga was loud as usual. I introduced them to Omy and Saitoti, the hotel owners. I bragged that I knew the who-is-who in town, and Oga laughed loudly and said that was why he had introduced me to another set of who-is-who to make my short list longer. We excused ourselves and went to our reserved gazebo outside.

Everyone was tired, but we needed to stretch the day some more because the trio was leaving for Nigeria that night. *Fufu* was served. It looked delicious, and I looked forward to tasting this famous Nigerian dish. I served first. Oga told me that it was also called *akpu*, meaning cassava. All along, I thought *fufu* was mashed Irish potatoes. I could smell something fermented as I served the off-white, smooth, elastic *fufu* with some soup and fish. Everyone was waiting to see my reaction after my maiden taste. It had a sour flavour to it, and I liked it. I didn't realise that the chef and his team were standing right behind me. They all clapped the moment I took my first bite.

After dinner, I quickly grabbed my notebook and asked numerous questions. Namrata and Patel were happy to assist. They were glad to be part of my journey. Soon, it was time to leave. Driving home, I thought about the three women who positively influenced Patel's company. I was also very grateful to Oga for the welcome surprise of introducing me to the Patels. I was too pumped to sleep that night. I decided to read through the notes I had written during my evening meeting with Namrata.

Should family enterprises be entrusted to women as their leaders? I was amazed at Patel's quick response. He said that women have a way of putting everything together. They have

> *Women have a way of putting everything together and bringing harmony among their employees.*

a way of ensuring things run smoothly. They brought harmony among their employees. They were the glue and grease at the same time. Patel said that his lovely wife, Namrata, had developed a structure with a clear chain of command. This significantly contributed to keeping business at SFC financially healthy and stable. Namrata interrupted and said that if SFC had not opened its doors to Patel's mother, his grandmother, and herself, major strides might not have been made. At Patel's Summer Fruit Company, I had the opportunity to indulge in the accounts of the contribution of Patel's wife, Namrata, his mother, and grandmother, albeit in absentia. These were three great women. What more could I have asked for?

What do transformational leaders do? Oga, who had been silent for some reason, responded that transformational leaders were progressive, intentional, and determined to make things work. Transformational leaders motivated and became role models to their followers. They encouraged teamwork. They ensured that their teams were well-coached and mentored. Oga thought Namrata fit in those shoes quite well, and Patel affirmed Oga's thoughts.

The only challenge with being transformational, Namrata said, was that we sometimes want so much change too soon. And before the change happens, we come up with another change. This had, at times, left her employees confused. She had to intentionally put down the changes she thought should happen, share them with Patel, and then they would write down the change process. This would provide a sense of focus and stability for everyone.

We all agreed that women were naturally transformational. Oga indicated that when teenage girls delivered children, they did not need to go to school to learn how to raise their children. Their natural motherly instincts would keep the child well-fed, encourage them to make a first step, and stimulate them to keep moving until they can run. The mother would act as a coach in potty training and as a role model to the child, even as they learned their mother tongue. All these were traits of transformational leaders which were inherent in women. This was quite profound. Oga's analogy made me think that if women could do all these great things for children, how much more could they do for family businesses? Push the enterprises to growth mode! This children analogy had come up a second time in discussions and this was fascinating.

beyond the border

I was beginning to see some common denominators with businesses that involved women in their leadership and this was very exciting. I was on a bus heading to Uganda one night to meet my friend, Claire. It had been a while since we met. I also needed some fresh air from the hustle and bustle of life, and traveling works wonders for me. The journey was smooth despite a few noisy Kenyan students who I assumed were traveling back to school from holiday who were a nuisance. I wished I had booked the seat next to the driver; it would have been quieter, or at least I thought so.

I got to Kampala at 4.00a.m. on a Sunday. Claire was supposed to pick me up at 4.00p.m. I was not sure what to do with all that time. I was tempted to check into a hotel room, freshen up and take a nap. On second thought, I decided to grab some breakfast in one of the city hotels since I had slept enough in the bus. I checked into a 24-hour hotel, the Bustani Hotel and Restaurant. I ate mashed matoke, fish slices, and vegetables served with tea. This was traditional, healthy, and quite filling.

With my confident God-given nature, I picked up a conversation with the waitress. I am so glad I did. It turned out the hotel belonged to her mother. I quickly grabbed this opportunity to fill in my usual curiosity. Would the positive impact of having women lead in family businesses in Kenya be similar beyond borders? My newly-found friend was Peace. She was a short, light-skinned, pretty girl with a round figure. I thought she looked like a doll. Her deep, authoritative voice did not match her stature. She was dressed in the waitress's uniform; a maroon, black and white kitenge shirt, with a short white skirt. She wore maroon high heels to complement her height.

Peace had worked at her mother's hotel as a waitress for three weeks. She was on vacation, and this would be her last working day since she was going back to school. She was at the university, studying hotel management. Her dream was to take her mum's business to another level.

The hotel had been inherited from her late grandfather, Mkisa. He only had one child, Precious. It was initially a tiny eatery with rooms hired out to other people to run different businesses. Her mother, Precious, renovated the place and pulled down some walls, creating a huge restaurant on the ground floor. She then put up an additional two floors. Mr. Mkisa would have been in shock had he decided to wake up from his peaceful eternal slumber. Things were totally different. Peace organized for me to meet her mother after church.

It was 8a.m. already. I decided to walk to the nearby Namirembe Anglican Church for the morning service. The cathedral was a sight to behold. I had visited the church fifteen years earlier during an exchange program. Therefore, I knew my way around. Peace's mother, Precious, was in the same service, but I did not recognise her. One, however, couldn't miss the short, round woman, dressed in a blue and white printed kitenge. She led the women's song and dance. She was as flexible as a riding whip. Her voice, a deep alto, was like that of a middle-aged, vocally experienced angel. She smiled, all her teeth out, as she ululated loudly in joy. The other women responded by clapping in a well-practised rhythm. One just couldn't help noticing her.

 It was a refreshing service. The preacher of the day happened to be a clergyman I had met at a training for church leaders in Kenya. I was excited to meet him again after the service. He reminded me of the topics I had taken their class through. 'It is surely a small world!' I thought.

I had an appointment with Peace and her mother at the hotel. I quickly dashed out and walked back. I was glad that Peace had been gracious enough to store my luggage. Walking up and down with a heavy black bag full of Pishori rice meant for Claire would have been hectic. She loved Kenyan rice. Back at the hotel, Peace was patiently waiting for me. We walked into her mother's office. Peace warned me that her mum was not going to keep time. She was a sanguine who would ensure she had spoken to all the women in the choir before returning to the hotel. Sure enough, Precious arrived thirty minutes later. I was shocked to discover that the dance leader, whose zeal I had admired at church, was, in fact, Madam Precious. I felt like I had known and conversed with her before. It turned out that she had noticed me too. I was seated at the front, dressed in trousers, an uncommon dress code for Ugandan women on Sundays. She confessed that she had looked for me after the service to give me a small lecture on my dress code, but I was lucky I had left already.

We bonded very well. The office was full of laughter. I was eager to hear what her business journey looked like. Her dad, Mkisa, was a hardworking man. He had bought a piece of land in his early twenties and put up a structure with rental rooms. He used the savings from his job as a gardener in a white man's home. He must have been very industrious. He took one of the rooms and made it an eatery when he retired in his late fifties. His customers loved his huge mandazis - one was enough to keep a traveler full on a journey to Mars.

Before he died at seventy, he handed over the hotel and rental rooms to his daughter, Precious, who had worked at the eatery for years as a waitress and cook. She decided to turn the whole structure into a hotel. It expanded a hundredfold. She introduced me to all the staff members, from the manager to the waiters, waitresses, and chefs. She had an amazing team. Precious took me upstairs to get a feel of the rooms. She was wooing me to make the hotel my go-to place anytime I was in Kampala. The rooms were spacious, modern, and had a touch of class.

We walked back downstairs to her office. I noticed that the restaurant was packed to the brim. All the waiters and waitresses were busy, either serving the seated customers or packing take-away food for those standing. The three chefs were as busy as bees. I had wondered why they needed three chefs when the employee introduction was done earlier. I now knew why. They were actually in the process of recruiting two more. I offered to assist them with conducting the interviews the following day.

I had so many questions running through my mind. While at Precious' office, Peace requested to be allowed to join her busy colleagues. I was impressed by her sense of responsibility. Precious was passionate about franchising the hotel business or opening several other branches. She committed to make the effort to reach some milestones toward expansion within six months. I believed her. Her resolve was iron-strong. Her zeal was not only in church but also in business. Most of her customers were church members who faithfully passed by for a Sunday package. The slogan on the package was 'Why cook? It's a Sunday, don't hassle!" No wonder the long queues. She had made people believe that Sunday should be a lazy day. No one should bother cooking.

> *Precious treated her employees with respect, professionalism and precision, ensuring that everyone verbalized any instructions given to them in her presence so that they did not achieve anything below her expectations.*

Precious treated her employees with respect, professionalism, and precision. She ensured that everyone verbalized any instructions given to them in her presence so that they did not achieve anything below her expectations. This made me think of why transformational leaders were considered very good communicators. They ensure that the intended message was the message that was delivered. She was firm, respectful, and motherly.

Friendliness, kindness, and cleanliness were the hotel's core values. She ensured that these core values were not just three words written on the wall, but a lifestyle everyone at the hotel lived by. A customer and employee feedback box had been placed in the washrooms. Any feedback received was taken very seriously. She joked that the gent's feedback box had been empty over the years and that the person in charge was always rated zero. The performance appraisal form offered five marks for handling washroom feedback conclusively. The employee responsible for the feedback box in the ladies' room got some marks quite often. Most of the feedback received was positive.

> *She was firm, respectful and motherly. She ensured that these core values were not just three words written on the wall but a lifestyle everyone at the hotel lived*

The hotel offered birthday parties exclusively for people over fifty years of age. These were full of song and dance, with special traditional meals for this health-conscious age-group. These parties kept the older generation attached to the hotel. The youngsters, too, had a room where they could watch 12D movies. I thought these were perfect strategies to attract and retain customers. No wonder the customers were a mix of all age groups.

It was 4.00 p.m. already, and Claire was waiting for me at the entrance. I bid Precious goodbye. I waved at Peace on my way out and confirmed that I would join her the following day to assist with the interviews for the chef positions. This was my way of appreciating their help in gratifying my curiosity. On my way out, I bought some lazy day dinner packages for Claire's children. It was an amazing Sunday with an unexpected free learning experience. This 'women thing' had crossed borders.

My one-week stay with Claire and her family in Uganda was amazing. The interviews for two additional chefs at Precious' hotel went very well. Peace had already left for school, but I was sure she would be thankful when she returned to find professional chefs with knowledge of international cuisines. This would help them attract the international community in Uganda. I needed to get back home and organize a meeting with the Heads of Department from the different organizations I had interacted with. I boarded a bus and headed back to Kenya.

cocktail meeting

I needed to make conclusions on various issues. The best team to help me develop a conclusive write-up was a blend of leaders from different organizations. Njeri, Becky, and Emmah had accepted my request to send their Heads of Department to a joint meeting. I communicated with Saitoti and Patel, and they were also willing to release their top cadre employees. Saitoti and Omy would host us for a cocktail party at their hotel.

The team was made up of five leaders from Wanjihia Lighting Company, sixteen HODs from Becky's firm, five leaders from Emmah's School, four leaders from Saitoti's hotel, and twelve heads of department from Patel's Summer Fruits Company. Precious' team from across the border was too far to get on board. Forty-two leaders from five different sectors was a significant number to have in one room. The common denominator was that their organizations were family-owned businesses that had women at their helm.

I got to hotel Ole Lenala at half past three. Saitoti and Omy looked very excited. I sensed that they wanted to be part of the whole story. But there was more - they revealed that all the ladies from the different organizations had been at the hotel since morning helping to organize the cocktail.

The well-manicured garden had ten well-dressed high tables about my height. When I moved closer, I realised that each table was under a parasol with beautiful bulbs labeled Wanjihia Lighting Company. These were from Njeri. Each table had jugs with various types of juices and cans of different fruits labeled Summer Fruit Company. These were from Namrata. She was already back from Nigeria.

I walked to the left corner of the garden and saw a whiteboard and marker pens, and I could tell that these were from Emmah's Ham Group of Schools. By this time, my tears flowed freely, messing up my makeup. There was a table set with all sorts of snacks, which were obviously from Omy's kitchen. I later learnt that Becky had donated the flower arrangements. The little white palm-sized bags at the extreme right corner were packed with painkillers, antacids, and mosquito repellants. The mosquito repellant came in handy that night since we remained outdoors.

I needed to dash to the washroom to wash my face. The love and sacrifice from the ladies were overwhelming. As I walked back, I noticed a reserved table inside the hotel. It had a ten-layer cake and a giant card with the words, "Thank You" written on it. Without much thought, I walked past it, back to the garden. The teachers from Emmah's school were the first to arrive. Within ten minutes, everyone was present. For some reason, I had a cocktail of feelings, nervous, excited, exhausted, and relieved that the job

was finally done. The cocktail meeting began with a word of prayer led by the Ham Group of Schools' high school principal. We were free to serve our juices, fruits, and bites as we introduced ourselves. Every table had a blend of four to five guests from different organizations. It was great seeing them bond freely. It seemed that they knew that growing networks was the way grow one's net worth.

I called the informal meeting to order. The objective was to illuminate the contribution of women in leadership in family businesses. I requested a volunteer to make short notes on the whiteboard. Every table was asked to list great things women in leadership had contributed to within their organizations. They were then requested to rate the contributions and narrow them down to the one they thought had the greatest impact. This way, I was assured of ten major contributions. We decided to number the tables from one to ten.

Table one: Encouraging creativity and innovation
Table two: Role modeling, hard work, and dedication
Table three: Coaching and mentoring

Table four: Motivating staff by rewarding good performance

Table five: Creating a structure, processes, systems, and documentation

Table six: Proper use of networks

Table seven: Creating alliances and collaborations

Table eight: Communicating expectations

Table nine: Allowing teams to think through issues for viability before implementation

Table ten: Genuine concern about employee welfare

I realised that the ten contributions relied on the skills associated with the female gender. After thanking the team for the priceless job well done, everyone received a token. It was a bracelet inscribed with the words, "I am enough, I have what it takes to succeed." This was meant to remind all of them to keep moving no matter what life threw at them. Everyone was then free to leave at their pleasure.

Omy gestured to me from inside the hotel. I was still in the garden, enjoying the snacks. I walked into the hotel, and she pointed at the table with the cake and giant card written, "Thank you". It was my gift from her and Saitoti! I was lost for words. They were grateful that I had connected Omy to a mentor who had assisted them in changing how things were running at the hotel. I was humbled. The waitresses had to assist me in carrying the mega cake to the car.

As I drove home, I thought I would sleep like a baby that night. I was feeling fulfilled. Oops! I was wrong. Thoughts of areas where women in leadership needed to improve came to my mind. I decided to take time and write down a few.

1. *Budget for a donation kitty. This reduces spending the organization's money on acts of mercy at the expense of business stability.*

2. *All transformational leaders, irrespective of their gender, should take time to plan for changes and allow teams to think through the change process. However, there should be a balance to avoid an analysis paralysis situation where opportunities are lost due to over-analyzing. The 'what if' question by women should not derail them from acting.*

3. *Encourage employees to contribute to a welfare kitty that would be a fallback in case of unforeseen challenges. Women in leadership should not feel obliged to sort out everyone's issues every time. The burden should be shared by the whole team.*

> *Take time to plan for changes and allow teams to think through the change process.*

4. *There is a need to acquire business skills and not only rely on women's inborn traits to succeed in business. A cocktail of both is vital for success.*

shouldn't she?

I was unsure of how to conclude this book. I switched on my laptop and just stared at it. I was seated at a restaurant, waiting for a friend I hadn't seen in a while. She became the spark I needed. Jane was in a huge family establishment. We had an appointment to discuss some business ventures. As we talked, I realised that her worldview was an eye-opener. She opined that, at some point, the top management should go out there and look for business and leave the teams they have mentored to handle the operations. This was the only way to grow a family business. In her case, she enjoyed being out there looking for more and more business. With proper processes, systems, and structures, the top management would be filled in on operational occurrences in real time.

Women in leadership should endeavour to grow their family businesses to the point where their main key performance indicator becomes hunting for and bringing new business on board. This is a sure way to grow the business market share, step by step.

1. Shouldn't she, then, be at the helm of family businesses?
2. Shouldn't she, then, be given some space to exercise her inborn transformational skills?

3. Shouldn't she, then, be intentional about mentoring her daughters, sisters, granddaughters, cousins, sisters, and nieces to be the QUEENS and PILLARS of family businesses?

Let's do it, ladies!